Lives and Times
Ludwig
van Beethoven

Peggy Pancella

Heinemann Library
Chicago, Illinois

Designed by Lucy Owen and Bridge Creative Services
Originated by Modern Age Repro
Printed and bound by South China Printing Company

10 09 08 07 06
10 9 8 7 6 5 4 3 2 1

Library of Congress Cataloging-in-Publication Data
Pancella, Peggy.
  Ludwig van Beethoven / Peggy Pancella.
    p. cm. -- (Lives and times)
  Includes bibliographical references (p.   ) and index.
  ISBN 1-4034-6746-3 (library binding - hardcover)
  1. Beethoven, Ludwig van, 1770-1827--Juvenile
literature. 2. Composers--Germany--Biography--
Juvenile literature. I. Title. II. Series: Lives and times
(Des Plaines, Ill.)
  ML3930.B4P36 2005
  780'.92--dc22
                              2005004197

Acknowledgments
The author and publishers are grateful to the following
for permission to reproduce copyright material:
AKG-Images pp. **9**, **21**; AKG Images/Beethoven-Haus
Bonn pp. **5**, **6**; AKG-Images/Erich Lessing p. **13**;
Alamy/GUS p. **26**; Alamy/Lebrecht Music and Arts
Photo Library p. **10**; Corbis/Archivo Iconografico, S.A.
p. **16**; Corbis/Bettmann pp. **8**, **17**, **18**; Corbis/Hulton-
Deutsch Collection p. **22**; Corbis/Reuters p. **27**; Getty
Images/Hulton Archive p. **15**, **24**; Karen Littlewood
p. **7**, **12**, **23**, **25**; Mary Evans Picture Library p. **20**;
The Art Archive/Museen der Stadt Wien/Dagli Orti (A)
pp. **14**, **19**; The Art Archive/Museo Bibliografico
Musicale Bologna/Dagli Orti (A) pp. **4**, **11**.

Cover picture of Ludwig van Beethoven reproduced
with permission of Corbis. Photograph of music
manuscript reproduced with permission of Corbis.

Page icons by Corbis

Photo research by Maria Joannou and Virginia
Stroud-Lewis

Every effort has been made to contact copyright
holders of any material reproduced in this book.
Any omissions will be rectified in subsequent
printings if notice is given to the publishers.

Contents

Introducing Ludwig van Beethoven   4

An Unhappy Childhood   6

New Teachers   8

Vienna at Last   10

Fame and Fortune   12

Hard at Work   14

A Difficult Man   16

Life Gets Quiet   18

More Changes   20

New Kinds of Music   22

Ludwig's Last Days   24

The Music Goes On   26

Fact File   28

Timeline   29

Glossary   30

Find Out More   31

Index   32

Some words are shown in bold, **like this**. You can find out what they mean by looking in the glossary.

Introducing Ludwig van Beethoven

Ludwig van Beethoven was a great **musician** and **composer**. His life was often hard, but he let his feelings come out through his music. Even when he became **deaf**, he wrote beautiful music.

Some people think that Ludwig was a **genius** because of the great music he wrote.

Ludwig lived in Europe at a time when many changes were happening. There were wars and new rulers. There were new ways of doing things. Ludwig wrote music that showed some of these new ideas.

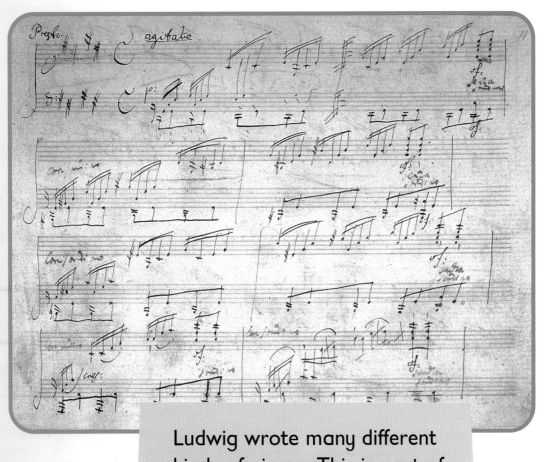

Ludwig wrote many different kinds of pieces. This is part of his famous *Moonlight Sonata*.

An Unhappy Childhood

Ludwig was born in Germany on December 16, 1770. His parents had seven children, but four died when they were young. Only three boys survived. Ludwig was the oldest.

The house where Ludwig was born is now a museum.

Ludwig left school when he was eleven. He never learned to spell or to do math well.

Ludwig's father taught his son to play the piano and violin. He was very **strict** and got mad when Ludwig made mistakes. Ludwig also went to school, but he did not do well.

New Teachers

Ludwig started studying music with Christian Neefe at about age ten. He practiced the piano and **organ**. Ludwig also learned to **compose**. Soon he got a job as an **organist**.

Neefe taught Ludwig to put his feelings into the music he played and wrote.

Mozart liked Ludwig's music. He **predicted** that the boy would become great.

In 1787 Ludwig went to Vienna, Austria. He had some lessons with the famous **composer** Wolfgang Amadeus Mozart. But soon Ludwig heard that his mother was dying. He hurried home.

Vienna at Last

Ludwig stayed home for five years. He went back to his **organist** job. He gave music lessons to earn extra money for his family. He also **composed** music when he could find the time.

Many artists and musicians went to Vienna. The people there supported their work.

Ludwig hoped to study music again. He got his chance when the **composer** Franz Joseph Haydn came to town and agreed to teach Ludwig. In 1792 Ludwig went to Vienna to work with Haydn.

Ludwig thought Haydn had too many old-fashioned rules about music.

Fame and Fortune

Ludwig played music at parties to earn money. He put a lot of feeling into his music. Sometimes he played so strongly that he broke the piano strings! People loved his exciting new **style** of music.

Ludwig loved to take long walks in the country. He got some of his best ideas for music there.

Prince Karl and his wife loved music. They both played the piano as well.

Soon Ludwig became very popular. He gave concerts and **composed** new music. Prince Karl Lichnowsky liked Ludwig's music very much. He invited Ludwig to live with him.

Hard at Work

Ludwig liked being famous, but it was hard work. Each morning he woke up early to **compose**. He often worked all night as well, going without food or sleep.

Ludwig often walked through town. Can you see him in this picture?

Ludwig was more interested in music than in cleaning. His house was always a mess.

Ludwig kept so busy that he did not take good care of himself. His clothes and hair were always messy and dirty. Once the police put him in jail because they thought he looked like a tramp.

A Difficult Man

As Ludwig grew more popular, many people wanted to become his friends. But Ludwig was not easy to get along with. He was often rude and grumpy.

Ludwig's friends wanted him to cheer up. They tried to get him to take better care of himself.

Ludwig did keep some close friends. He fell in love several times, too. None of the women would marry him. So he just worked harder than ever on his music.

Ludwig wrote music and letters to women he loved. This is part of a love letter he wrote.

Life Gets Quiet

When he was about 30, Ludwig started having trouble hearing. Sometimes his ears buzzed. Sometimes he could not hear nearby sounds. He could not even hear his own music. Ludwig felt afraid and angry.

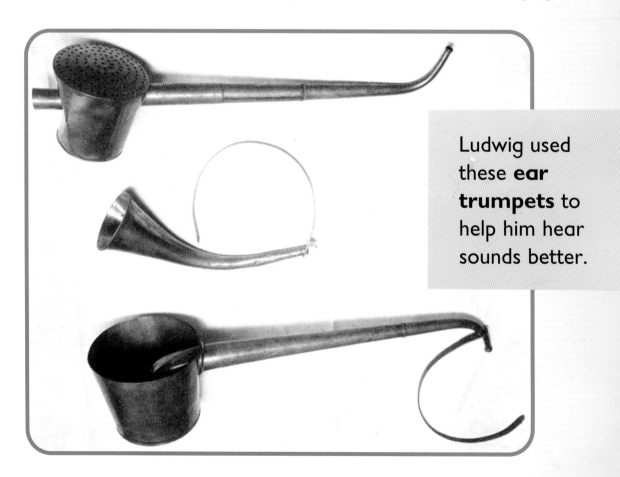

Ludwig used these **ear trumpets** to help him hear sounds better.

While in the country, Ludwig wrote a long letter to his brothers. He explained his feelings about going **deaf**.

Ludwig spent a summer in a quiet country village. He was very lonely and sad, but his music cheered him up. He was still able to imagine sounds in his head. He could still **compose** music.

More Changes

Ludwig's new music was very powerful. He wrote longer pieces with many dark feelings. But times were changing in Europe. People liked light, pretty tunes better. Ludwig's new pieces were not very popular.

Ludwig's strong music was hard for people to understand.

One of Ludwig's brothers died, leaving a son called Karl. Ludwig wanted to raise young Karl. Karl's mother wanted the boy to stay with her. She and Ludwig fought over Karl for years.

Karl was about nine when he came to live with his uncle, Ludwig.

New Kinds of Music

By 1818 Ludwig was totally **deaf**. He still tried to write good music for people to enjoy. His newest pieces were hard, but they sounded beautiful. People grew interested in his music again.

This is a performance of Ludwig's only **opera**, which is called *Fidelio*.

One of Ludwig's last pieces was his Ninth **Symphony**. He stood on stage watching the **orchestra** play. But he could not hear the music. He thought no one liked it because he could not hear clapping.

Ludwig turned around to see the cheering crowd. He began to cry with joy.

Ludwig's Last Days

Ludwig was glad that people liked his new music, but life was still difficult. His nephew Karl grew upset and ran away. Then Ludwig became very ill. He could no longer **compose**.

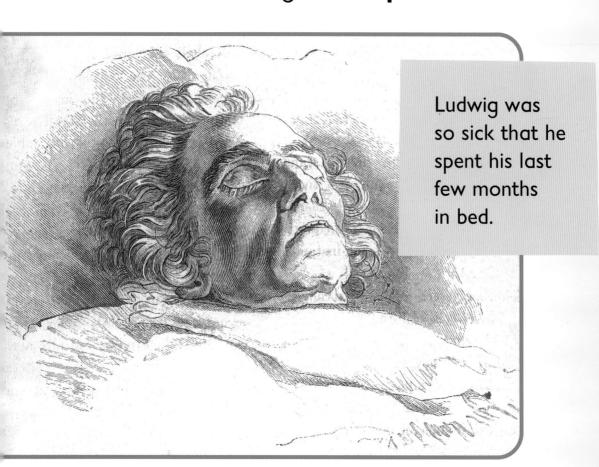

Ludwig was so sick that he spent his last few months in bed.

Huge crowds came out to say goodbye to the man who wrote such beautiful music.

On March 26, 1827, Ludwig died. He was 56 years old. The schools in Vienna were closed on the day of his funeral. About 20,000 people came out for his funeral **procession**.

25

The Music Goes On

Ludwig's life was hard in many ways, but that did not stop him from writing great music. He put his feelings into the music he **composed**. He tried different **styles** of music. He worked in new ways.

There are many statues of Ludwig in Europe. This one is in Vienna.

Today, Ludwig's music is still very popular. His works are played and sung around the world. A recording of one of his pieces was even sent into space on the *Voyager* spacecraft.

Ludwig's *Ode to Joy* uses a large **choir** and **orchestra**.

Fact File

- Ludwig was known for his bad cooking. He liked to make strong coffee, macaroni and cheese, and mushy soup with eggs and bread.

- Sometimes Ludwig **conducted** his own music. He often waved his arms wildly. He jumped up during loud parts and bent low during quiet parts. Sometimes he shouted without knowing what he was doing.

- The European Union (EU) is a group of countries in Europe. They try to work together. The EU chose Ludwig's *Ode to Joy* as its **anthem**. The words of the song are about people being peaceful, free, and equal.

- Ludwig died during a powerful storm. One story says that he heard a huge clap of thunder. He opened his eyes and shook his fist at the sky. Then he lay back and died.

Timeline

1770   Ludwig is born in Germany on December 16

1775   Ludwig begins music lessons with his father

1784   Ludwig gets a job as an **organist**

1787   Ludwig studies with Mozart; Ludwig's mother dies

1792   Ludwig meets Haydn and goes to Vienna

about 1798   Ludwig first notices problems with his hearing

1802   Ludwig spends a quiet summer in the country

1805   Ludwig finishes his **opera**, *Fidelio*

1815   Ludwig's brother Kaspar Karl dies; his son Karl moves in with Ludwig

1818   Ludwig is completely **deaf**

1824   Ludwig finishes his Ninth **Symphony**

1826   Karl runs away; Ludwig becomes very ill

1827   Ludwig dies on March 26

Glossary

anthem song of praise or gladness, often having special meaning to a person or group

choir group of singers

compose to make up music

composer person who makes up music

conduct to lead or direct a group of musicians

deaf unable to hear

ear trumpet object that is held up to the ear to help a person hear better

genius person who is unusually smart or good at something

musician person who makes music

opera play with words that are sung, not spoken

orchestra musical group that contains many different instruments

organ keyboard instrument that makes many different sounds, usually by pushing air through pipes

organist person who plays an organ

predict to tell what will happen in the future

procession people moving along in an orderly line or group

strict firm and forceful

style way of doing things

symphony long piece of music written for many musical instruments to play together

Find Out More

More Books to Read

Cencetti, Greta. *Beethoven*. New York, N.Y.: Peter Bedrick Books, 2001.

Lynch, Wendy. *Beethoven*. Chicago, Ill.: Heinemann Library, 2000.

Turner, Barrie Carson. *Ludwig van Beethoven*. North Mankato, Minn.: Chrysalis Education, 2003.

Places to Visit

There are many places in Europe that honor Ludwig today. These include:

Ludwig's birthplace, Bonn, Germany
Beethoven Memorial Museum, Vienna, Austria
Bourdelle Museum, Paris, France.

In the United States, one college has a large collection of Ludwig's works:

Ira F. Brilliant Center for Beethoven Studies at San José State University, San José, California.

Index

childhood 6–8
composing 4, 8, 10, 14, 19, 20, 22, 26
conducting 28

deafness 4, 18–19, 22
death 25, 28

ear trumpets 18
European Union (EU) anthem 28

family 6–7, 9
Fidelio 22

Haydn, Franz Joseph 11

Karl Lichnowsky, Prince 13
Karl (nephew) 21, 24

love letters 17

Moonlight Sonata 5
Mozart, Wolfgang Amadeus 9

Neefe, Christian 8
Ninth Symphony 23

Ode to Joy 27, 28
opera 22
orchestras 23, 27
organ 8, 10

piano 7, 8

Vienna 9, 10, 11, 25
violin 7
Voyager spacecraft 27